New PLAYS

EASTERN STANDARD
BORDERLINES
AMULETS AGAINST THE DRAGON FORCES
THE MAGIC ACT
KILLERS
THE DEATH OF PAPA
IMPASSIONED EMBRACES
CLEVER DICK
LOVE MINUS
BIG MARY
FAITH, HOPE & CHARITY
ELECTION YEAR & SO WHEN WE GET MARRIED
TWO EGGS SCRAMBLED SOFT & A BRIEF PERIOD OF TIME

Photo by Stan Sadowski

David Hurst and Anthony Chisholm in a scene from The Wilma Theater production of "Incommunicado." Set design by Andrei Efremoff.

INCOMMUNICADO

BY TOM DULACK

DRAMATISTS
PLAY SERVICE
INC.

SPECIAL NOTE

All groups receiving permission to produce INCOMMUNICADO are required (1) to give credit to the author as sole and exclusive author of the play in all programs distributed in connection with performances of the play and in all instances in which the title of the play appears for purposes of advertising, publicizing or otherwise exploiting the play and/or a production thereof; the name of the author must appear on a separate line, in which no other name appears, immediately beneath the title and in size of type equal to 50% of the largest letter used for the title of the play, and (2) to give the following acknowledgement on the title page of theatre programs and on all billboards, posters and other paid advertising (1/8 page or larger in which the producer credits itself) for the play, on a separate line as follows:

"Originally produced by THE WILMA THEATER, Philadelphia, Pa."

(3) to give the following acknowledgement in the theatre program:

"The Wilma production was awarded a major grant from the Fund for New American Plays, a project of the John F. Kennedy Center for the Performing Arts with support from American Express Company in cooperation with the President's Committee on the Arts and Humanities."

"The poem "Erat Hora" by Ezra Pound from PERSONAE (Copyright 1926 by Ezra Pound) is used by permission of New Directions Publishing Corporation. All other quotations from Ezra Pound used by permission of the Trustees of The Ezra Pound Literary Property Trust and New Directions Publishing Corporation, agents for the Trust."

SOUND EFFECTS

An audio cassette containing the sound effects which may be used in connection with the production of this play, can be obtained from Thomas J. Valentino, Inc., 151 West 46th Street, New York, N.Y. 10036.

For my wife, Véronique

INCOMMUNICADO had its world premiere at The Wilma Theater (Jiri Zizka, Blanka Zizka, Artistic/Producing Directors; W. Courtenay Wilson, Managing Director) Philadelphia, Pennsylvania, on February 28, 1989. It was directed by Blanka Zizka; the set design was by Andrei Efremoff; the costume design was by Lara Ratnikoff; the lighting design was by Jerold R. Forsyth; original score was by Adam Wernick; and the stage manager was Kathryn Bauer. The cast was as follows:

EZRA POUND .... David Hurst
MP .... Anthony Chisholm
TILL .... Reginald Flowers
LAWYER .... Peter Wray
DOCTOR .... David Simson

The Wilma Theater production was subsequently performed at the Kennedy Center for the Performing Arts (Marta Istomin, Artistic Director) Washington, D.C., in July, 1989, and was presented as a co-production. The cast was as follows:

EZRA POUND .... David Hurst
MP .... O.L. Duke
TILL .... Reginald Flowers
FORBES .... John Michael Higgins
DR. MULLER .... Edwin C. Owens

A NOTE ON LANGUAGE

Pound speaks in the play in a variety of accents. He goes from High British to uneducated Deep Southern, to Midwestern. He hides behind these accents and mimickry; it's a way of defending himself, concealing himself. His mockery of the MP is often in the very voice of Rochester on the Jack Benny radio program, or Amos and Andy. The switching of voices, accents, languages, is part of his virtuosity. The more this happens in the play, the greater the variety of verbal effects achieved, the better.

INCOMMUNICADO

ACT ONE

In darkness, an impersonal Voice begins to read the Indictment.

VOICE. The Grand Jurors for the United States of America duly impaneled and sworn in the District Court of the United States for the District of Columbia and inquiring for that District upon their oath present: That Ezra Pound, the defendant herein, was born at Hailey, Idaho, October 30, 1985, and that he has been at all times herein mentioned and now is a citizen of the United States of America and a person owing allegiance to the United States of America. *(Lights up gradually on a cage made of heavy-duty air strip welded over galvanized mesh, just large enough for a man to stand up in and lie down in, a kind of oversized dog kennel, one of a row of cages housing condemned military criminals in the middle of a prison yard of the Detention Training Center, Mediterranean Theatre of Operations, U.S. Army, on a hill above Pisa, Italy in the hot spring of 1945. Inside the cage the prisoner, Pound, comes visible in shadowy outline and bulk. We do not see into the other cages. It is night. The reading of the Indictment continues without interruption.)* That the defendant, Ezra Pound, at Rome, Italy, and other places within the Kingdom of Italy and outside the jurisdiction of any particular state or district, but within the jurisdiction of the United States and of this Court, the District of Columbia being the district in which he was found and into which he was first brought. *(Enter a black MP who shines a flashlight into Pound's cage.)* Continuously and at all times beginning on the 11th day of December 1941, and continuing thereafter to and including the 3rd day of May 1945, under the circumstances and conditions and in the manner and by the means hereinafter set forth. *(The MP leaves.)* Then and there being a citizen of the United States, and person owing allegiance to the United States, in violation of said duty of allegiance. *(The MP returns*

carrying a length of fire hose which he attaches to a hydrant.) KNOWINGLY. INTENTIONALLY. WILLFULLY. UNLAWFULLY. FELONIOUSLY. TRAITOROUSLY. AND TREASONABLY. Did adhere to the enemies of the United States, to wit; the Kingdom of Italy and the military allies of the said Kingdom of Italy, with which the United States at all times since December 11, 1941, and during the times set forth in the indictment, have been at war, giving to the said enemies of the United States aid and comfort within the United States and elsewhere. *(Moonlight now, the compound walls are visible, concentration camp details of machine gun towers and barbed wire. The MP aims the fire hose into Pound's cage and turns on the water. Pound shrieks. We see him thrown back against the rear wall of the cage by the force of the water, impaled on it, crucified, arms flung out to either side. The MP turns the water off, Pound collapses. The MP leaves. There is a pause. Then Pound stirs, crawls forward, and not realizing the MP is gone, speaks into the darkness.)*

POUND. I think there must be some mistake. I don't belong here. The name is Pound. P.O.U.N.D. As in Of Flesh. Poet. A.K.A., also known as, The Great Bass. *Il Miglior Fabbro,* Gospel according to Eliot. I'm sure it's a procedural matter, a legal technicality, clear it up in no time. If I could just see a lawyer, clear it up in no time, count on it, bet on it. *(Calling.)* Hey, you! Hey, Buck! Hey, Kingfish! Hey, Rochester! I've got my rights, you hear me, boy? You can't execute a man without a trial and unless things changed since I been out of the country, you can't have a trial without letting me consult with an advocate. Even the United States Army can't execute an American citizen without providing him with legal counsel. *(The MP returns, silent, big, all menace and institutional brutality. He takes up a position to one side of the cage and does not look at Pound. In a shift, fearing another water assault.)* Anyway, at least a pencil and a scrap of paper. You see, I don't have any writing implements. None of the tools of my trade. What do you say, Sergeant? Think you could work on some paper and a couple pencil stubs for Ole Ez? Problem is, I've got no time, Sergeant. And there's so much to do. Maybe you can't appreciate that a man on death row can have a need to do things. But there's all the more reason, being on death row. I have so much still to say, so much imagining to do. See? That's my job. Imagining.

It's what I do ... *(A siren erupts. The MP gives a start, tenses but doesn't move. There are shouts in the distance, whistles. A searchlight explodes across the yard sweeping back and forth. There is the sound of large dogs barking. Then short bursts of machine gun fire. After which, silence.)* Anybody ever make it over the wall, Jim? Anybody ever make it out of here in one piece? To the best of your — using a term loosely — knowledge? *(The MP doesn't answer. He moves around the cage, takes up a position on the other side. He conveys the impression that he is somehow tentative, curious even, though very hostile.)* Sneaking admiration, though, admit it. For the gallantry. The sheer desperate gallantry of the attempt. Desperate men. You ever think of it that way, Jim? You're in a fair way to become an authority on the inner workings of the souls of desperate men. Could write a book some day, if you could write, hey, Jim? Ever get that shameful itch in your loins? Ever wonder what it's *like,* Jim? Ever lie there at night dreaming about plunging your bad old utensil into that forbidden honeypot? Your prehensile utensil? Hey, Jim? You be careful. Keep your pants buttoned up, Jim. Look where writing got *me.* It's where it gets all of us. Five minutes of pleasure and then a lifetime of clap, take my word. My Word! My words. What do you say, Jim? You can't shoot a man without first he writes a last will and testament.

MP. You ain't supposed to talk! You got no privileges. You're bein' held incommunicado and that means you ain't supposed to talk. It's against the rules for you to talk!

POUND. It's a question of velocity. I've lived my life at a tremendous velocity, a tremendous intellectual velocity. My brain *spins,* Jim, it whirls, it careens. The inside of my skull is a regular velodrome. There's a lot of centrifugal pressure that needs to be relieved. I gotta formulate me some words, friend, I gotta write, you gotta let me write, else I'm going to die.

MP. Die. *(He marches off, boots crunching. Pound watches him go, then sits cross-legged, his head lowered in submission and resignation.)*

POUND. We learn from Confucius in the *Analects* that: Yi was a mighty archer, and Ao shook the boat. Yet both of them came to a bad end. *(He is silent. It is very dark, then a searchlight beam stabs into his cage from above and to the right. Then another, like a lance, from the left. Then two, three more, Pound fixed as if skewered by the*

shafts of light. There is a beat, and then fierce sunlight, frying the cage. Pound groans, gasps, we can hear his heart beating. The MP enters, drenched with sweat. Pound begins to recite in a harsh croak lines from the Cantos.) Io venni in luogo d'ogni luce muto. The stench of wet coal. Politicians E. and N., their wrists bound to their ankles.

MP. Shut up, Pound, you are forbidden to speak.

POUND. Politicians addressing crowds through their ass-holes. Addressing the multitudes in the ooze.

MP. I said shut up, Pound!

POUND. Profiteers drinking blood sweetened with shit. *(The MP suddenly tugs his service automatic from his holster and aims it at Pound's head.)*

MP. I'm warning you, mother fucker! I wouldn't hesitate! *(There is a long moment, Pound staring unblinking into the mouth of the gun.)*

POUND. And speaking of shit, Sergeant, how about a pot in here and a scrap of toilet paper? Nothing fancy, I've lived most of my life in Europe, I don't crave convenience, any old back issue of *Stars and Stripes* or the stray corn cob will do nicely. And maybe an old coffee can for the deposit of unruly feces, I don't require luxuries.

MP. You love your slop and shit, Pound. *(He returns the gun to the holster.)* You're worse than a fucking animal. Live in your own filth. I wouldn't waste an American bullet on you.

POUND. Be that as it may, could I trouble you then to bring me some information about my wife and children. I have an aged mother living in Rapallo. Also a friend named Olga Rudge. Could we just send a word out that I'm alive, tell 'em that I'm well.

MP. It's against regulations.

POUND. But it's torture for them, it must be torture. No one knows where I am.

MP. That's right, nobody knows, and nobody cares, and that's how it's going to stay.

POUND. But why punish them? They haven't done anything. They're innocent. Just let them know I'm alive. Is that asking too much?

MP. Yeah. It's asking too much. *(The MP starts to leave.)*

POUND. At least get word to my mother! She's not well, the strain can kill her! Jesus, have a heart, Sergeant!

MP. Mister, just consider yourself buried alive! *(And he marches off. Pound after a moment urinates out the back of his cage. The stream of urine judging by his reaction spreads toward the neighboring cage.)*

POUND. Hey, watch it down wind! Hey! Piss call! Sorry, sorry, you guys. Sorry amici, sorry neighbors. Nothing personal. You just happen to be unfortunately situated: "downhill of the poet's foetor," down-wind of the poet's stink. *(He listens for a reply. There is none.)* Anybody home over there? Anybody home? No? Nobody home? Sorry. Sorry. *(He sinks down into a huddle in a stupor. After a moment he begins mumbling. Then we hear that he's reciting lines of his own verse, in a monotone, like a litany.)*

"The blowing of dry dust and stary paper.
Foetor, sweat.
The stench of stale oranges.
Dung.
Last cess-pool of the universe ..."

(He is silent, the lights go to black, it is night, the searchlights comb the yard. The MP enters with a tin dish, a dog dish, with some scraps of meat and bones in a watery gravy. He unlocks the door of the cage, dumps the mess unceremoniously on the ground, closes the door but does not lock it, and leaves. Pound, on his hands and knees, gnawing at the bones.) The danger lies in adopting *their* point of view. The danger is to concede they may have a point. A pencil is potentially a lethal weapon. You could enter through an eyeball and plumb the depths of your brain with a sharpened pencil. The same with a spoon, even a spoon. A cup, a dish, a toothbrush. Got to reject all that. What passes for their thinking. I want to enter *their* eyeballs, plumb their brains with my pencil. And I damn well am going to do it too. Concede nothing. Concede fuck all! *(He finishes his meal, and with a sigh leans his head against the door of the cage which swings open silently. He simply stares at it for a long moment. Everything is still and silent, the searchlight does not appear. After a pause, Pound slowly creeps forward, advancing with great caution, filled with fear, wonder, tension, as if expecting each new movement might trigger a catastrophe. Finally he is completely outside the cage. He stands up, looks around disbelieving. In the distance a dog barks. Pound looks around, calls softly to the other cages.)* Hey! Hey, anybody home over there? No? Yes? *(He cautiously advances on the neighboring cages and*

looks into them one by one.) Empty. Ditto. No one home. *(He returns to his own cage, stands in front of it, tests the air, sniffing, like an animal scenting danger.)* Nobody. Nothing. Where's the searchlight? Smells like a set up. Fuck you, Jim! *(And he crawls back inside and closes the door.)* Fuck you, boy. They don't call me The Great Bass for nothing. *(And he curls up and goes to sleep. A beat. Then with reveille piping across the yard through loudspeakers, there is full light. The Orders of the Day are read on the P.A.)*

P.A. VOICE. Orders of the Day:
The Officer of the Day is Lt. Fletcher.
Working Company is Abel.
Duty Section is Section 2.
Working parties will be called away at ten hundred and 1430 hours.
Muster with Sgt. Timmons in front of the Main Gate.
Reminder First Army's Inspector General is due Fifteen June.
Battalion Commander will inspect Barracks "A" today.
Sunrise tomorrow will be at 0546 hours.
Today's note from the Judge Advocate: discussing classified information with uncleared personnel is an offense subject to non-judicial punishment. *(The MP enters, jerks open the door of Pound's cage.)*

MP. Out, Pound! On your feet. You got exercise privileges. Fifteen minutes a day. Out, out, out!

POUND. *(Like a German.) Raus, raus, raus!* I ain't movin' Bub, until I get a pen, paper, a toothbrush, a cup, a spoon, and a pot to pee in.

MP. You come out of there or I'm coming in after you.

POUND. I prefer not to.

MP. I'll break your neck, Pound! Come on out of there!

POUND. Ah, but you see, Jim, that would be a self-contradiction wouldn't it? The reason the government of my country refuses to permit me to eat with a spoon, write my poetry with a pencil, clean my teeth with a brush, is a self-admitted concern for my corporal well-being. The government intends to hang me, so you can't break my neck, Jim, without committing a very grave act of insubordination. On the other hand, you ain't gonna induce Ole Ez to exercise — to get himself in shape for the hanging — *unless* you break his neck. But I remain amenable to reason,

Jim. What you need from me is 15 minutes of exercise. What I need from you is a toothbrush. The situation is fraught with the potential for collaboration. *(The MP suddenly dives into the cage and drags Pound out.)*

MP. Get your ass on outa there! Now exercise! *(Pound stands motionless, smiling at the MP.)*

POUND. Confucius tells us in the *Analects* that a gentleman can be broken, Jim, but you cannot dent him. *(And he sits, arms folded, at the MP's feet. The MP stares down at him, fists clenched in helpless fury. Then blackout. When the lights come up again, the two men are in the same relative position, but Pound is now holding the toothbrush the MP has just presented him, and a tin cup of water. An ecstatic smile is on his face. He begins to brush his teeth as though it were the most luxurious, even voluptuous act he has ever performed. He gargles for a long time, rinsing his mouth. He spits, suggestively. Then he carefully places the cup and the toothbrush in a corner of the cage as if he were hoarding treasure, smiles cheerfully at the scowling MP, and begins to perform a series of calisthenics. Blackout. Night. From Pisa, above the camp, a churchbell sounds midnight. Very dim light on the row of cages. In a hoarse whisper.)* Till? Till? You there?

TILL. *(Whom we never see, just a voice from the adjoining cage.)* Yeah, Grampaw, I'm here. You there?

POUND. Seem to be.

TILL. You *all* there, Grampaw?

POUND. *(A cackling laugh.)* Not bad, Till, really not bad. I most certainly have been accused time to time during my life of not being all there.

TILL. Why ain't you asleep?

POUND. Can't sleep.

TILL. Why not?

POUND. Working.

TILL. Working!

POUND. Writin' a poem.

TILL. In the dark?

POUND. Easier to see.

TILL. Without no paper?

POUND. Don't have to worry about erasing my mistakes. Where you from, Till?

TILL. St. Louis. Where you from?

POUND. Idaho. But I also did time in Indiana.

TILL. Indiana.

POUND. *(Hums some bars from a song like "Back Home Again in Indiana.")* Crawfordsville. Did six months of hard labor at Wabash College, Department of Romance Languages. Moonlight on the Wabash. Moonshine on the Hogwash. Lived in a boarding house owned by a couple of spinsters. The Misses Hall. Got fired as a result of the moral intervention of the good ladies who took umbrage at my sheltering a homeless girl I found in a blizzard. Oh it was terrible sad, Till, I tell you terrible sad. I gave her my bed, an act of pure compassion. But the Misses Hall didn't see it that way. They chose to place an evil interpretation on the event. They telephoned the president with their dire intelligence and the next day I was gone. The girl too. In separate directions, I hasten to add. I'm writing a poem about hell. Giving Crawfordsville a whole circle all to itself.

TILL. You sure can talk, Gramps. I bet you got yourself a whole lotta trouble with that mouth of yours.

POUND. And what got you into trouble, Till? Certainly not poetry. What are you in for?

TILL. Murder and rape. With all the trimmings.

POUND. Don't concede the bastards a damn thing, Till. Give 'em nothing. It's the only way to survive.

TILL. Hey, Grampaw, I did it. I told you. With all the trimmings. And I mean *all* of 'em! Ain't got nothin' *not* to give 'em. Ain't gonna survive, Gramps. Gonna hang. And probably a good thing. For everybody. Yep. Probably a damn good thing. What you in for, Gramps?

POUND. Mistaken identity. Soon to be rectified. I have no doubt. Which is to say, they got the wrong man.

TILL. They never get the wrong man Gramps.

POUND. Conviction of innocence only thing sustaining me, lad.

TILL. You ain't guilty, you wouldn't be here, Pops.

POUND. Grave errors of procedure. Endemic to a bureaucracy.

TILL. Naw, you're guilty, old man. You are guilty. You wouldn't be here otherwise. Nobody'd be here they weren't guilty.

POUND. In other words you're reconciled to being hanged?

You view that event with equanimity?

TILL. Look, they's only one way you leave these cages, Gramps, and that's in a box. Man, don't you understand? Don't you understand where you are?

POUND. The first thing to do is subvert and demoralize the conqueror. You have to make the conqueror a victim of his own violence. You have to infiltrate their consciousness, Till. You'll see.

TILL. It's better you just admit it, Gramps. Better you just come out and admit you're guilty.

POUND. You'll see.

TILL. Lot better for everybody involved.

POUND. You'll see.

TILL. I'm telling you. *(Pound is silent. The sound of a church bell. Then lights up and Pound is doing exercises under the critical scrutiny of the MP who sits on a packing crate chewing gum and spitting from time to time. Winded, Pound stops, sits sprawled, trying to catch his breath.)*

POUND. Fifty.

MP. *(Involuntarily.)* Forty-nine.

POUND. *(Scrambling to repeat the last exercise one more time.)* Fifty! Feels great to be alive, Jim, you know that? Trouble with the intellectual life, we don't get enough exercise. Everything depends on the supply of blood to the brain. You probably can't guess by looking at me, but I used to be a pretty fair athlete in my day. Tennis, used to love playing tennis. *(He begins to mime a tennis game.)* Backhand never much good. But I was always quick on my feet. Still am. Fancy footwork covers up a lot of mistakes. I can see you're surprised there's so much bounce in me still. *(He mimes a serve and a backhand volley.)* Fancy footwork. Same principle in tennis and in boxing. You follow the fights, Bo? Brown Bomber, credit to his race. Credit to *your* race, Bo. But Mr. Billy Conn is a case in point. Speed of foot will always neutralize brute strength. *(He begins shadow boxing.)* Come as a surprise to you, but I studied the art of pugilism with one of the greats. Mr. Ernest Hemingway taught me everything I know about pugilism. Come on, Bo, let's go a few rounds, what do you say? *(He flicks some taunting jabs close to the MP's unbelieving face.)*

MP. You gotta be kidding.

POUND. No, come on, it's a lot more interesting and instructive for both of us. *(He dances around the MP shooting out hooks and jabs.)* Come on, what do you say, what's the matter, you afraid I'll make you look bad?

MP. *(Standing.)* Oh boy! *(He removes his gun belt, Pound strips off his shirt; he is wearing only baggy pants, his feet are bare. He dances, feints, bobs and weaves.)* Oh boy!

POUND. Hem used to call this hooking off the jab. *(He throws two ludicrous punches, and the MP swiftly strikes him in the face twice with an open hand.)* Or maybe you're supposed to jab off the hook. Hem used to say you had to slide off the punch. *(The MP almost contemptuously knocks him down with a single blow.)* Ah, that was a beauty, Jim. You have a certain — how shall we say? — native aptitude for pugilism, anyone ever tell you that? *(He gets back shakily to his feet.)* Bob and weave. Superior speed and intelligence will always neutralize ... *(The MP knocks him down again.)* God, your hands are so quick, Jim! You really ought to turn pro. You're even better than Hemingway. *(He gets back on his feet.)* Okay, giving you fair warning, I've just been toying with you, Jim. *(He launches a pathetic, staggering attack, flailing ineffectively, which the MP parries effortlessly, and then he hits Pound with a flurry of punches to the midsection that drops him again.)* Great! Beautiful! A pleasure to watch! *(Hoisting himself to his feet again.)* But you know what Confucius says. When ornament prevails over substance, you get the pedantry of the scribe. *(Pound falls in a heap and does not move. MP goes off, comes back a moment later with a bucket of water. He sloshes it over Pound who stirs. Kneeling, the MP pulls him into a sitting position, mops the blood from his face with his shirt.)*

MP. Just tell me one thing, why did you do it, Pound? WHY DID YOU DO IT?

POUND. Why did I do what?

MP. Why'd you sell our country down the river?

POUND. I didn't sell anybody down the river.

MP. They say you're a traitor.

POUND. I'm innocent, Bo. I didn't betray anybody. *(They are frozen like that for a moment, Pound in the black MP's arms, and then a fade to black. In the darkness Till's harsh whisper.)*

TILL. Hey, Gramps! Can you talk? *(It's too dark to see Pound who*

replies weakly, in pain.)

POUND. Think I've got me a deviated septum, Till. Have to let Hemingway know his tutorials didn't cover all contingencies. Still, it's safe to say I converted him.

TILL. Converted him!

POUND. I'll turn him into a blasted aesthete before I'm through with him. Make him an apologist for Western Civilization. The moment you begin to praise a savage for his savagery, he ceases to be a savage. He becomes introspective. And that's the beginning of the end. You'll see, Till. I've got him on a short leash now. Next thing is to get a muzzle over his snout so he can't bite. After that, it's only a matter of time. I'll have him walking on his hind legs and whistling "Dixie!"

TILL. What the hell you talking' about Gramps?

POUND. I told you I'd subvert him. I won him over. He's mine now.

TILL. Won him over! He damn near killed you!

POUND. Small enough price to pay to save the world.

TILL. Save the world? You fixin' to save the world, Grandpaw?

POUND. Make it safe for poetry. Here is my body, take ye and beat. *(He laughs.)* Whataya say, Till? Somebody's got to save the world, might as well be me. Not that the goddamned world deserves saving. I could be forgiven for harboring a grudge. If not against the planet entire, then at least against that corner of it that gave me suck, as it were. Drove me out and barred the gates, Till. Informed me in no uncertain terms the NATION didn't need my brand of filth and pornography parading around disguised as highbrow poetry. They kicked me out, Till. And now look at the deal of trouble they're taking to bring me home again.

TILL. The man called you a traitor, Gramps. That what you in here for?

POUND. No.

TILL. Treason, Man. I mean treason. Treason is bad shit!

POUND. You love your country then, Till?

TILL. Naturally I love my country. Don't you?

POUND. Yeah, I love the old bitch. But as Alexander the Great said of his mother one time — she charges a bloody high rent

for nine months lodging! *(Quotes.)*

And I was desolate and sick of an old passion,
Yea, I was desolate and bowed my head:
I have been faithful to thee, Cynara! in my fashion ...

But *your* fidelity to Old Mistress Quickly is a singular affair, Till. Your country wants to hang you after all.

TILL. Hey, Pops, what the hell kind of country would it be if it *didn't* want to hang someone like me? I wouldn't want nothing to do with a country put up with scum like me. You gotta hang me. They's nothing else to do with me. It's just like that. But treason is somethin' else. Yes or no? Is that what you're in here for?

POUND. I'm innocent of what they said I did, Till. That's enough for you to know.

TILL. You swear you're innocent?

POUND. Or there's no such thing as innocence.

TILL. *(After a pause.)* That sounds like a fishy answer to me.

POUND. It should. It comes from the Great Bass, way down in the deep. The deep. Shall we look for a deeper, friend? Or is this truly the very bottom? *(The MP enters in dim light. We can only see him, nothing else. He takes a harmonica out of his pocket and plays. He plays several bars, a blues melody. Then he leaves.)* A goddamned Orpheus now! What did I tell you. He's practically courting this old Hell Dog, Till. *(In the distance, a harmonica picks up the same tune the MP was playing, then fades, as light develops, full day, and Pound revealed with the door of his cage wide open, him seated outside, his back against it, a bandage on his nose, writing in a notebook. The MP enters, is annoyed.)*

MP. Don't you ever do nothin' else but write? What the hell you writin' all the time in there? What the hell you got to *say?*

POUND. Want to go a few rounds, Orpheus?

MP. Naw, it ain't no fun boxing with someone like you, can never learn.

POUND. Hemingway said I had a gift.

MP. Hemingway was wrong.

POUND. He often was. But I know exactly what you mean. I felt the same way trying to teach poetry to my Hoosier knuckleheads. They'd sit there all white and motionless in their serried

ranks like so many tombstones. Know exactly how you feel. Nevertheless, I regret my incompetence. I was having a good time.
MP. Getting the shit beat out of you?'
POUND. Wonderful sense of liberation. Total submission to the Powers That Be. Sense of fatalism. Everything out of my hands. *(He writes for a few moments.)*
MP. You're a weird old coot. Lemme see that. *(He snatches the notebook and stares at it.)* What the hell *is* this? What is it?
POUND. Chinese. Give it back.
MP. You write in Chinese?
POUND. When the mood is on me. When I don't feel like writing in Greek, or French, or Russian. Now give it back.
MP. What's it say?
POUND. Go learn Chinese and then you can read it for yourself.
MP. How do I know this ain't some secret message in some kind of code?
POUND. It *is* a secret message in some kind of code. Otherwise called poetry. Damned if you ain't a critic all of a sudden. Get me locked up with a bunch of nigger rapists and murderers and what do I find but my jailer is an art critic, wouldn't you know! Now give it back before you get your disgusting paw prints all over the thing.
MP. Watch yourself, old man, I'll kick the shit out of you you don't watch that big mouth of yours.
POUND. I don't have to worry about that anymore, Bo. You already pointed out the logical fallacy of beating up on a man don't know how to defend himself. Now, give it to me!
MP. What if I don't. What if I rip it up?
POUND. Then you'll force me to write it all over.
MP. What if you can't remember?
POUND. Ain't a question of *remembering*. It's a question of *seeing*. All I got to do is close my eyes and I see the poem. It's there, like a picture on a wall.
MP. It's just hanging there? Just like that?
POUND. Just like that.
MP. I don't believe you. Go ahead show me. Close your eyes and tell me what you see.
POUND. How? You don't understand Chinese.

MP. You think you got all the answers, don't you? Well what do you think of this? *(And he begins ripping pages from the notebook and shredding them. He chews on some, spits them out, scatters the pages wildly, stamps on them. Pound watches wary but impassive.)* What do you think of *that* for your fuckin' poetry?

POUND. I think you do a fair imitation of a caveman. Or a National Socialist. Or a U.S. Customs inspector reading Joyce's "Ulysses." Or an American publisher. Or a baboon in heat. *(MP grabs Pound.)* It's all here, just right in here, Bo. I told you. And you can't touch it. You can't touch me. Nobody can. See? I close my eyes and I'm gone. Venice, Florence, Rome. There's a boatyard across the canal from where I lived in Venice. Used to spend half the day watching them make the gondolas. Coming up out of the oily water, black and shiny, like prehistoric sea serpents. Been to Venice, yet, Jim?

MP. No. *(Pound on hands and knees crawls around collecting the shreds of his poetry.)*

POUND. Not to be missed. Famous New York journalist on assignment to Venice, arrives there for the first time, takes one look, sends a wire back to the home office: STREETS FLOODED, PLEASE ADVISE. *(Offering the MP a handful of shredded paper.)* Care for another mouthful? No? You've had your belly full of poetry for the day. Your C-ration of Literature, is that it, Tom? *(He swallows a mouthful of paper.)* Mmmm. Delicious. A little salty though. The Word made Flesh, Bo! That's the ticket. Fucking sacrament this. *(Offering another page from his notebook.)* A little dessert? One for the road? No? Mind if I do? *(And he eats it and wipes his beard fastidiously as if he'd just finished a large meal.)* Let me know when you're going to Venice. I'll give you some letters of introduction. Florence too, you don't want to miss Florence. Fine sense of corruption and moral decay in Florence. Something gross, something carnal in the air, a miasma comes up from the river like poison. Especially in the summer. The summer heat *incites* a man, Bo. They tell the story of Cosimo the First went round the bend one day and had his own daughter as they say in the Good Book. They could hear her screaming for miles around. Even the statues are filthy. Donatello, Michelangelo. Bunch of pederasts, Booker T. What

else? I wasn't surprised the Germans tried to blow the joint up when they left. An act of belated morality. Down with pornography! Whataya say, Booker T.? *(He eats some more of his poetry.)* Gives new meaning, don't it, to the idea of a man eating his own words.

MP. Sometimes I think you belong in a booby hatch.

POUND. You think somehow the Great Bass is more a prisoner than you are, Tom? Don't kid yourself. We're in this thing together, you and me. Which is as it should be, being as we are, members of the same fraternity, so to speak. The poetic fraternity, I mean.

MP. Poetic fraternity!

POUND. What else is that wild fire in your eyes if it ain't poetry, soldier? It's what attracted you to me from the start. Oh-oh, I told myself, here's a fellow toiler, a fellow-sufferer, a fellow laborer in the vineyards.

MP. What are you talking about?

POUND. The Miglior Fabbro is never wrong. You're a man obsessed with images, could tell at a glance. Where'd you spend your last weekend pass? Don't tell me, let me guess. Down in the Campo Santo lost in a reverie before the great Fresco of the Last Judgement by The Master of the Triumph of Death!

MP. I spent my last weekend pass in a cathouse.

POUND. Amounts to the same thing. I always thought there was a certain elective affinity between a cathouse and a poem. Closest thing a lot of people ever get to poetry, a piece of ass, I always felt. Closer than a lot of "poets" of my acquaintance ever got.

MP. Ain't you afraid at all?

POUND. Afraid of what? Why should I be afraid?

MP. That you're gonna die.

POUND. *(Collecting and smoothing some of the crumpled and torn sheets from the notebook, arranges himself just inside the entrance of his cage and begins to write.)* Consolation of religious philosophy. Buddhism. Tell you something, Soldier. The Ego is the arch-fiend. Don't forget that. Once you circumvent the Ego, the energy of the Universe becomes available to you. Fact. It's like plugging into a Universal Power grid. You become a conduit for

the great galvanic current that animates the vortex. Anything is possible, everything's a miracle. Look at this wasp. You ever see anything like it? The miracle of waspishness. This ant. This spider. There's a cat comes round at night sponging off the prisoners. I hear the roosters at dawn, the pies, the wrens and martins and meadowlarks. I could just as well be St. Francis as ole Ezra Pound. Heightened sensibilities. So intense! At times I'm like a tuning fork, I swear: I vibrate. A mosquito can set up a sympathetic vibration along the length of my vertebrae. You could play Bach on my spinal column time to time, Buck. Pound the Well-tempered Clavier! No room for fear of death in this instrument. Too much life inside this cage.

MP. *(Hesitantly, after a pause again.)* This ain't my idea, you know.

POUND. What ain't your idea?

MP. Keeping you living like this.

POUND. Never said it was.

MP. It's orders, that's all. I'm only obeying orders. You're not even supposed to have a pencil.

POUND. *(Without apparent interest.)* Much obleeeged! —

MP. Just so you know. *(Pound writes.)* They find out you got a pencil and paper from me, I'd be in a lot of trouble.

POUND. Right. Inasmuch as I'm officially the enemy now. You could be found guilty of aiding and abbetting the enemy in time of war yourself! You know the penalty for collaborating with the Occupying Power in time of war?

MP. What "occupying power?"

POUND. Me! I'm the Occupying Power in your brain right now, Jim. And you gotta keep resisting me, you want to be a credit to your race. You're a candidate for one of these death cells yourself, you ain't careful. See how narrow this definition of "treason" can become in the wrong hands. Flirtin' with it yourself. How a little charity can bring a man down in this world. How's it feel, Jim, this clandestine foray into the world of counter-intelligence? Relax, Sergeant, your secret's safe with me.

MP. What secret?

POUND. That in your insubordinate heart of black hearts you are resisting the Official Party Line that says I am a traitor.

MP. No, I suppose you are a patriot. Tell me you're a patriot

now, Pound.

POUND. Don't bet against that, Jim.

MP. The government's got you cold, Old Man. They got you dead to rights.

POUND. They got *you* dead to rights too, ain't they? In the eyes of the majority of our fellow countrymen there ain't a dime's worth of difference between some poor no account nigger like yourself, and some poor no account VERSIFIER like me. It explains this otherwise mystifying sympathy you're feeling for me. Deep down you *know* I'm just another colored boy, far as the US guv'ment is concerned, with their heel in my face! Just like you. They assign you to keep an eye on me, me to keep an eye on you. They kill two birds with one stone. Now get the hell out of here. I got to work. And lock the door. I don't want to be gunned down by some goon who can argue later I was trying to escape. Remember, as Confucius tells us in the *Analects*: The hen pheasant of the hill bridge knows how to bide her time. *(He settles down to write. The MP slams the door of the cage, locks it, and stalks off. A moment later he reappears.)*

MP. I'm gonna BRING you another notebook, mother-fucker!

POUND. It's the least you can do. *(Blackout. The sound of distant thunder. Then the sound of rain. In the dark Pound calls out.)* Till? I'm adrift.

TILL. You gotta ask 'em to dig you a ditch, Gramps. They make a leach field for the water to run off. Only don't send it down this direction. I got enough to worry about. *(Dim light on the cages.)*

POUND. What you got to worry about, St. Louis Till? Aside from keeping your plumbing dry.

TILL. Approaching death in so many words, Grampaw.

POUND. What approaching death? You're gonna live to be a hundred.

TILL. Nope. I got the feeling it's gonna be soon. Little thangs. The way somebody looks at you. The way somebody *don't* look at you. Like everybody *knows* 'ceptin' you.

POUND. It's your imagination, Till. Relax. Take it from the Great Bass. We're wearing 'em down, kid. Be out of here in no time.

TILL. Huh-uh. It's gonna be soon, Pops. I kin tell.

POUND. I tell you we're wearing 'em down. It's strictly a matter of staying power. Any day now they'll capitulate.
TILL. I ain't got long, Gramps. This nigger ain't got long ...
(No lights. The rain subsides. Silence. Then full sunlight and Forbes, an army lawyer, a Lieutenant, enters smartly, sets a folding chair down in front of the cage and opens a briefcase.)
FORBES. Dr. Pound? I'm Artemis Forbes. I'm here to provide you legal counsel.
POUND. *(Writing.)* Just a minute, Buster. I'm tryin' to put the Post-War World in some kind of shape to listen to reason. Tryin' to talk some sense into that primitive Mongolian brain of Joe Stalin. Can you mail this for me?
FORBES. You're writing to Stalin?
POUND. Stalin, Churchill, Tojo. Let me give these birds 20 minutes of grade school economics and there won't be any more wars — ever. If anybody is interested, you tell 'em to come see Ole Ez. Drop this in the mail for me?
FORBES. I'm sorry, I'm sure it's against regulations.
POUND. If it wasn't against regulations, Sonny, I wouldn't be asking you to do it, would I?
FORBES. I can't mail your letter.
POUND. Well, if you're writing to him yourself, send along my regards. What did you say your name was, sonny?
FORBES. Forbes.
POUND. No, your first name.
FORBES. Artemis.
POUND. Artemis! Good classical moniker. Greek goddess. Twin sister of Apollo. Call you Artie?
FORBES. You can call me whatever you want, Dr. Pound.
POUND. Oh yeah? How about I call you Honus Wagner then? A particular favorite of mine, Honus Wagner. The Old Flying Dutchman. You follow baseball, great baseball name you bear, there, son.
FORBES. Actually, I don't, I mean I haven't ...
POUND. You can call me Ezra, sonny. Il Miglior Fabbro. How's your Italian? It means "The Finer Craftsman." What about the Japs? They still fighting?
FORBES. I'm under orders, Dr. Pound, to help you prepare your

defense. I'm not at liberty to give you information about what's happening outside. In fact it's expressly forbidden.
POUND. *(Coughing.)* You from Massachusetts?
FORBES. *(Surprised.)* Yes, actually.
POUND. Accent's a dead giveaway. You read any of my stuff? You familiar with my crap? My Clap Trap?
FORBES. In fact, I'm afraid not, I don't read poetry.
POUND. I could tell you didn't. One glance I said to myself, this cookie ain't exactly your garden-variety Bloomsbury aesthete. But how you plan to defend me you're not familiar with my crap?
FORBES. Actually, I'm here to give you advice, not to mount a formal defense. You'll be tried in the United States. I'm here to help you evaluate your position, to determine what exactly your position might be at the moment relative to ...
POUND. *(Interrupting.)* To determine my position? My position is that of a dog in a kennel, Forbes. Once a day they throw some bones on the ground for me to gnaw. I eat and sleep in my own piss and shit. Once every 24 hours they flush me out with a fire hose. My neighbors are rapists and murderers. I grill in the sun and freeze under the stars. When it rains I have to try to sleep standing up. My gums are bleeding, I have diarrhea but they won't let me see a doctor. I'm not permitted to communicate with anybody, nobody's permitted to talk to me.
FORBES. Yes, I see. Well, but, unfortunately, I'm not at liberty to ...
POUND. You're not at liberty? Well where does that leave us? If *you're* not at liberty, Artie, who the hell is? If my attorney ain't at liberty, how the hell am I supposed to defend myself?
FORBES. I don't have the latitude, you understand, Dr. Pound. I'm constrained simply to note, to take note of the conditions that prevail relative to proposing ...
POUND. You're *constrained*, Forbes? You say you're constrained?
FORBES. A figure of speech, Dr. Pound.
POUND. Figure of speech! Imagine! Two minutes with the Great Bass and you're turning into a Bloomsbury aesthete after all, Artie. Better look out or Virginia Woolf will be inviting you to tea. You want to be careful with these figures of speech, sonny.

A power of trouble in a figure of speech. Look where figures of speech have landed me.

FORBES. Are you all right, Dr. Pound?

POUND. Ain't for me to say, is it? Ain't modesty at all for me to say I'm all right. Or not all right. Who am I to determine?

FORBES. No. I mean sick. Are you sick? You seem feverish.

POUND. Does my family know where I am? Do my children know I'm alive?

FORBES. I'm sorry, I'm not at liberty, I'm not free, it's not permitted ...

POUND. MOTHER OF CHRIST! *Do they know or don't they know?*

FORBES. I can't tell you, I don't have that information.

POUND. All right. All right. All right. Say what you got to say. What do you have to tell me? Let's get on with it.

FORBES. *(Referring to papers.)* This is just my opinion, of course. But I really don't think you can defend yourself with any reasonable chance of winning. So if I were you ...

POUND. How about an unreasonable chance of winning?

FORBES. I don't think you have any chance at all.

POUND. No? So what am I supposed to do? Cut my throat?

FORBES. I don't think you have a lot of choice. If I were you, I'd try to avoid letting this thing come to trial.

POUND. Avoid going to trial?

FORBES. That's right.

POUND. Negative.

FORBES. Negative?

POUND. *Non! Nyet! Jamais!* Forget it! The government's telling its side of the story all over the world. I want to tell my side.

FORBES. Look. I'm going to level with you. Whether you know it or not, you're in very deep shit. The government wants to hang you.

POUND. But I'm innocent!

FORBES. Each radio broadcast is being treated as a separate act of treason. There are 84 separate counts in that indictment.

POUND. There's not one word, not one syllable of treason in any of those broadcasts. It was a series of lectures on economic theory designed to put an early end to this war and to make sure we'd never have another one. I was against the war from 1932.

I saw it coming before anybody. It's a matter of record. I tried to tell Roosevelt what was what in 1939 but he wouldn't listen. By the time I got to Mussolini it was too late. You know damned well, Forbes, if I'd made those broadcasts on U.S. soil there wouldn't be any indictment for treason.

FORBES. For all I know, you're right, you're probably right.

POUND. I want a trial! I have a right to a trial! If they hang me, they hang me. What the hell kind of man would I be if I was afraid to die for what I believe?

FORBES. It's not a good idea. I wouldn't be doing my job if I didn't tell you that.

POUND. I'll take my chances. What kind of case they got? You think they got a case?

FORBES. It's not a question of what kind of case they have. I don't think you can get a fair trial.

POUND. Why not?

FORBES. With all this about the Jews? Not in that climate of opinion. Forget it, forget a fair trial. You don't have a prayer.

POUND. Jews! What have the Jews got to do with my trial? What are you talking about, Forbes? What is this climate of opinion?

FORBES. Look, why don't we continue this when you're feeling better?

POUND. What are you talking about!? What's going on over there?

FORBES. I'm talking about the concentration camps, the atrocities.

POUND. Goddamn it, what atrocities? What do I have to do with atrocities?

FORBES. You're telling me you don't know what happened at Dachau, at Auschwitz?

POUND. Where? What? I never heard of these places! What's this all about? *(After a moment of hesitation, Forbes opens his briefcase and takes out a newspaper.)*

FORBES. You're not supposed to see this, but how in the hell am I supposed to advise you? ... This is *Stars and Stripes.* The same thing's been showing for weeks all over America. Newsreels, radio, the press. Just filled with it. *(He passes the paper*

into the cage.)

POUND. *(Suspiciously.)* What's this? *(He squints at the paper.)* My eyes ain't what they used to be ... It looks like ... it looks like a mountain of ... what the hell? ...

FORBES. Bones.

POUND. What the hell is this?

FORBES. Those are skeletons. People. Most of them were Jews. Nobody knows how many. Millions. Up to six million was the last figure I heard. They were gassed and shot and cremated. In these concentration camps.

POUND. Jews ...

FORBES. Jews. Gypsies. Homosexuals. Communists.

POUND. *(Who cannot stop staring at the pictures.)* The Germans did this?

FORBES. They didn't self-destruct, Dr. Pound. Anyway, that's why you can't get a fair trial. People back home are really worked up about this, they want revenge.

POUND. *(Sickened.)* I didn't have anything to do with this.

FORBES. You have a history of Jew-baiting, Dr. Pound. Sorry, I don't know what else to call it. If we're talking legalisms, technically, no American's ever hanged for baiting Jews. I personally don't have anything against the Jews. But I know a lot of people in America, I know a lot of people in this Army, who are anti-Semites. I know Jews who are anti-Semites! Now these broadcasts, these transcripts, what I've seen of them, it's gutter talk, verbal sewage. I don't like it, it's not my speed, I don't dislike it. I've heard worse. Granted, only in bars and bowling alleys, but I've heard worse. But what you said or didn't say isn't the point. What happened to the Jews in these concentration camps has changed all the rules. We're putting Nazis on trial for crimes! This has never happened before. There's no legal basis for this, there's no precedent! In the United States of America, at the present time, in this climate of opinion, Jew-baiting has become treason! And that's what these people will focus on. They hate you, Dr. Pound, and you give them the chance, they're going to string you up. And American Justice can't protect you. You can't give this to a jury! You can't go to trial! Are you listening to me, Dr. Pound? I think your best chance is to plead guilty and throw

yourself on the mercy of the court. With luck, they'll give you a prison sentence.

POUND. Are you *crazy?* You're my lawyer, you're telling me to plead guilty? So maybe — IF I'M LUCKY, the man says — they'll lock me up for the rest of my life! If I'm lucky!

FORBES. I realize it sounds pretty drastic. But I really don't know what else you can do. You think about it for a few days and it might look a little better.

POUND. No soap, Forbes! God damn! This is some kind of American justice, ain't it? Giving me a lawyer whose best idea is to plead guilty! What the name of God I need some son of a bitch like you telling me *that?* Why don't you just give me some cyanide and be done with it? You a lawyer, Forbes? You a lawyer in civilian life? God help your poor damned clients! I want a trial. I have a right to a trial. I'm an American citizen. *(Getting progressively worked up until he's out of control.)* I'm an embarrassment to the U. S. Government, ain't I? Why don't you just admit it. Come sneaking in here trying to talk me into pleading.... Get out of here, Forbes! *(He thrusts the newspaper through the bars of the cage.)* Nobody's gonna pin this Jewish rap on me! I'm innocent, and I'll prove it in a court of law! They're afraid of me, ain't they? They're afraid to have me debate their conduct of the war in a court of public opinion. And they have good reason to be afraid!

FORBES. I'll come back when you're feeling better, Dr. Pound. *(Forbes starts to leave.)*

POUND. Wait a minute! Come back here! I ain't finished with you! I demand you get a letter to my wife! To my publisher. To the State Department! To Churchill and Stalin! *(Forbes goes out.)* Goddamn it, Forbes! Forbes! Forbes, come back here! *(But Forbes is gone. There is a terrific peal of thunder which seems to knock out the lights. A wind begins to blow.)*

TILL. *(In the darkness.)* They're doin' it in the morning, Gramps. They're gonna execute me. Firing squad.

POUND. What it is, St. Louis Till, is a conspiracy to discredit me. They're afraid of me, Till. They don't want the Great Bass writing any more. They think they can shut me up.

TILL. I'm leavin' instructions to give you my blankets after I'm

gone. If you don't mind wrappin' yourself in some dead nigger's blankets.

POUND. A man can live with a charge of treason win or lose. What the hell, look at Dante, they accused Dante. Blake. Galileo. For the love of God Socrates!

TILL. You think you could do me a favor, Gramps? You think you could write a letter to my Momma after I'm gone? I don't know how to write. Tell her ... tell her ... tell her I died in battle. Tell her I died like a man. *(He starts to cry.)* God, I miss my Momma. Will you write her a letter, Gramps?

POUND. I'm writing a letter to the President, Till. Test my influence in high places. Put in a good word for you too, don't worry.

TILL. It's too late for me. They'll be here any minute. God, I hope I don't shit my pants. Dear God, don't let me shit my pants!

POUND. Listen to this, Till. Dear Truman. Ezra Pound speaking from his Babylonian Captivity. Let's get this goddamned festering racial issue disposed of right off the bat, dispose of it once and for all. I submit to you, Herr True-Man, that from 1935 to the dismal present day, a conscientious and patriotic American citizen of the Christian persuasion and tempered by the Renaissance, a man like that — looking to his government for MORAL GUIDANCE on the burning question at hand — could never have guessed or otherwise predicted that anti-Semitism, *soi disant,* would emerge from this war-debacle as an indictable capital crime of treason! How the hell you birds in Washington justify something like that? How's it sound so far, Till?

TILL. I don't wanna die. I know I deserve it, I know I'm guilty, but, damn, I'm afraid, Gramps.

POUND. From 1935 to the DISMAL PRESENT no man could find MORAL GUIDANCE from his government by and for, and he couldn't find it from his culture neither, and that's KULCHER with a capital K, Buster! And God knows not from his blasted/blessed Church.

TILL. I wasn't afraid when we was fightin'.

POUND. Listen to this, Till. This is the good part.

TILL. I was in the middle of it, we lost our whole company

comin' up the peninsula.

POUND. Truman, they say you're a student of History.

TILL. Lost damn near every one.

POUND. So then you're probably well aware that from Time Immemorial the extermination of the Jews had Christian sanction.

TILL. I was decorated three times for bravery.

POUND. Christian. Christian sanction. Where am I? Some of the great, the great SCRIBES —

TILL. If I get my ass shot off in battle, I die like a hero. Same man, same black ass.

POUND. And Saints, Popes, even Popes and Fathers of the Church — from Time Immemorial — some of 'em went so far as to suggest ...

TILL. They give my Momma a medal, a 21 gun salute ...

POUND. Went so far as to suggest that GOD created the Jews in the first place to provide Christians with the opportunity to secure an improved, and upgraded level of habitation in the Great Hereafter *by exterminating 'em!*

TILL. It ain't fair, it just ain't fair, ain't right, ain't fair ... *(We hear Till crying.)*

POUND. I can't think straight, Till. This is important! Truman! Where am I? Quote. Pound speaking! Where, in the year of Our Lord nineteen hundred and forty something was a Christian American Man supposed to find moral guidance on this question of the JEWS? *(Thunder and lightning.)*

TILL. I didn't ask to be sent to Italy.

POUND. Can you tell me that, Mr. President? I hope you and your in-JUSTICE department can come up with some pretty good answers to this nettlesome question, because it's at the heart of the matter. And if you got no answers then how the hell can you hang a MAN?

TILL. They give you a gun, they teach me to kill.

POUND. Shut up, Till!

TILL. They teach me Dagos are the enemy.

POUND. How can they shoot you? How can they execute anybody?

TILL. It ain't fair, Gramps. It ain't fair, it just ain't fair.

POUND. It's a question of moral guidance! *(We hear the tramp of marching feet.)*

TILL. God, they're coming, Gramps!

POUND. Wait a minute! Wait a minute! *(We hear the order for the execution being read.)* You can't do this! Where is your sanction? *(We hear the neighboring cage being opened, Till sobbing, a priest intoning prayers in Latin.)* Stop ... stop it! Where is your moral authority? You can't do this! *(Sounds of scuffling and cries as Till is dragged from his cage. Someone saying, "Act like a man, soldier! Pull yourself together." Beginnings of a distorted Requiem.)* A presidential pardon is in the works! I'm writing to Truman, I'm writin' to Joe Stalin! This man's got CLEMENCY comin' to him! *(Till's screams retreating as the mingled sounds of storm, Requiem, heartbeats grow, buffeting Pound.)* Wait a minute! Come back! Where's your authority? You can't do this, you can't do this to a MAN! *(And he suddenly begins to wail the Kaddish as on the sound track we hear Pound also raving lines from "King Lear.")*

Blow winds, and crack your cheeks!
Rage!
Blow!
You cataracts and hurricanes spout!! —

(We hear a Requiem being sung. And then the singing of the Kaddish. Mixed with this is the ululating wail of an Arab religious cry, the wail of the Muezzin. The sound of marching feet. Muffled drums. Finally Pound gives a great scream, and collapses, and there is instant SILENCE. Blackout.)

END OF ACT ONE

ACT TWO

In darkness.

VOICE. FROM: FIFTH ARMY GROUP
TO: ALLIED FORCE HEADQUARTERS, Info G-5 For G-2
Awaiting orders for disposition from your Headquarters for DR. EZRA POUND, War Criminal. Please advise.

TO FOR ACTION: ADJUTANT GENERAL, WAR DEPARTMENT, WASHINGTON
SIGNED: EARL ALEXANDER, ALLIED COMMANDER
In custody Provost Marshal here is EZRA POUND.
Reference AGWAR cable of 14th May.
Investigation completed. Statement by POUND and documentary evidence airmailed FORNEY 21 May. Request information POUND's further disposition soonest. *(Lights slowly up on Pound seated in a chair next to a desk in an office. There is a flag, a map on the wall, a picture of FDR and of Truman. Pound is wearing a hospital gown. He seems drained, ruptured, haunted. He sits unmoving.)*

TO FOR IMMEDIATE ACTION: COMMANDING OFFICER, HQ MTOUSA
FROM: COMMANDER PENINSULA BASE SECTION, DTC
Reference War Criminal DR. EZRA POUND.
Request urgent attention to disposition of prisoner. Please reply ASAP. *(Enter Dr. Muller, an Army psychiatrist, middle-aged, congenial, sympathetic.)*

MULLER. Good morning, Dr. Pound. I'm Colonel Muller.
POUND. I'm sure you are.
MULLER. Well, you've had what our British colleagues would call "a sticky patch" of it, haven't you?
POUND. I've got nothing more to say to you birds.
MULLER. It helps to talk, Dr. Pound.
POUND. The other character said I was exhibiting abnormal pressures of speech. Seemed to hold it against me.
MULLER. There's nothing to be afraid of.

POUND. I ain't afraid.
MULLER. *(Explaining.)* You see, you were sick to begin with. Running a fever, undernourished, dehydrated. You were feeling stressed and fatigued. On top of that, the execution of Private Till was a terrible assault on your nervous system. Think of the nervous system as an army under siege.
POUND. *(Quoting.)* "I fish with a line but not with a net. When fowling I don't aim at roosting quail." *Hamlet.* Top-secret!
MULLER. That's not Hamlet, that's Confucius, isn't it? I was saying: The nervous system erects certain defenses against assault. What we call a "breakdown" is the system shutting down to protect itself. Our animal instincts take over in times of stress. We revert.
POUND. I do not revert ... *(Muller scans some reports.)*
MULLER. It says here you continue to run an intermittent low-grade fever.
POUND. That's a fair description of my life, ain't it? An intermittent low-grade fever.
MULLER. Are we getting that under control finally?
POUND. My low-grade fever or my low-grade life?
MULLER. Bowel movements?
POUND. Yes. In fact periodically since infancy.
MULLER. Color?
POUND. Of my infancy?
MULLER. Of your bowel movements.
POUND. Fuschia. Sometimes chartreuse.
MULLER. The color could be significant.
POUND. Go check the floor of my cage, see for yourself.
MULLER. We're just trying to help, Dr. Pound.
POUND. "Then they for sudden joy did weep
And I for sorrow sung
That such a king should play Bo-Peep
And go the fools among."
MULLER. In your delirium ...
POUND. *(Cutting him off.)* *What* delirium?
MULLER. You were delirious. And while you were delirious, you were speaking Hebrew.
POUND. That ain't very likely.

MULLER. Why not?
POUND. Ain't a language I know.
MULLER. Nevertheless.
POUND. Who says it was Hebrew?
MULLER. One of the orderlies in the hospital, he's Jewish. He says it was the Kaddish, the Jewish Prayer for the Dead.
POUND. Impossible.
MULLER. It's strange how we sometimes know things without knowing how we know them. Maybe when you were a child, you had school friends who were Jewish ...
POUND. I didn't have friends in school. Only admirers.
MULLER. You still have a lot of admirers. Even here.
POUND. Yeah? Well they seem to have mastered the technique of protective coloration. They blend in very nicely with the yellow clay.
MULLER. *(Reciting.)*

"— And then she turned
And, as the ray of sun on hanging flowers
Fades when the wind hath lifted them aside,
Went swiftly from me. Nay, whatever comes,
One hour was sunlit, and the most high gods
May not boast of any better thing
Than to have watched that hour as it passed —"

POUND. *(Surprised and moved.)* "*Make* boast."
MULLER. I'm sorry?
POUND. It's "make" boast of any better thing.
MULLER. Oh, right! *(Correcting.)*

"May not *make* boast of any better thing
Than to have watched that hour as it passed."

POUND. Yeah, well, there *was* one sunlit, hour, wasn't there? And it sure has passed.... Unusual for an American medical man to have a taste for poetry.
MULLER. I studied English for a while, music too, before I went into medicine. The University of Pennsylvania, in fact. Well after you were there.
POUND. C-plus. I'd give it a C-plus some kid in Creative Writing handed that to me. B-plus if it came from Wabash College.
MULLER. Who was the "she?" The "she" who turned away?

Was it someone in particular or ...

POUND. Who the hell knows anymore? All the women you once loved, and who you now hate, they all, one way or another become your Mother, don't they? My bowel movements are brown.

MULLER. *(Writing it down.)* Thank you.

POUND. It could have been Greek, I was talking.... The orderly in the hospital could have been mistaken.

MULLER. Do you understand the charges that have been brought against you?

POUND. Just so much flapdoodle!

MULLER. Would you like to discuss the charges?

POUND. Flapdoodle pure and simple, all of it.

MULLER. Do you feel responsible for the deaths of millions of Jews in the concentration camps?

POUND. No! Hell no! Why should I?

MULLER. What *do* you feel responsible for?

POUND. My work, my poetry, that's all.

MULLER. Might there be a relationship between your poetry and the broadcasts on Italian Radio?

POUND. *(After a pause.)* Yeah, there might be. There just might be ... *(He thinks.)* The thing about those broadcasts, Muller ...

MULLER. Yes?

POUND. There might be a relationship. It's all a question of images, isn't it? Images! You see you are being *broadcast.* Entirely new thing in poetry. To be broadcast. New thing under the sun. I was suddenly fashioning air waves! Never mind The Word Made Flesh. This was better. This was The Air Made Word! I was amplified! From now on, I thought, when you talked about poetry, you couldn't limit yourself to discussing iambs and strophes, similes and metaphors. It was a new age. When you talked about Poetry from now on, you had to talk about Kilowatts!

MULLER. Kilowatts?

POUND. Miraculous kilowatts! Absolute units of Power! Pure Power, possessing me, transforming me, flinging me like streams of tracer fire flashing out in great rising arcs across the Alps, across the Pyrennes, into the black reaches of the firmament — bearing my words, my voice, my image, transcending for the

first time in history the limits of a poet's mortal coil ... I was like Icarus on that first solo flight — this incredible expansion of the soul as he was uplifted towards the Sun ... *(Pause.)* Which waited impassively to cremate him.

MULLER. So then, when you're creating, when you're in the throes of artistic creation, it's analogous to flight? You experience a sensation of flying?

POUND. Leave the Renaissance alone, that's my advice. You start out taking a pleasant little promenade, Sunday afternoon, harmless little picnic in the woods. And before you know it, you're headfirst down The Rat Hole, plunging upside down into the very universal CENTER of things. And in the very molten center is a lake of ice, and that's the heart of God. And in the center of the lake of ice, chewing on Judas Iscariot for all eternity is the Big Fella.

MULLER. *(After a moment.)* Fascinating! Could we explore that Hole, that idea of plunging down the Hole. It's the womb, isn't it?

POUND. It's Dante.

MULLER. Yes, but it could have been the womb for Dante as well. The womb or the anus.

POUND. *(Heaving a sigh.)* That's all, Brother. I got nothing more to say.

MULLER. Our time's up anyway.

POUND. You birds just about finished with me?

MULLER. Oh, far from it, Dr. Pound! You're a very interesting case. You see, a man of genius is to a psychiatrist what a man with testicles is to a eunuch.

POUND. Oh yeah? Well, tell your buddies I ain't leasing out my testicles. They ain't for hire. Tell 'em to grow a pair of their own. Tell them when I'm dead, they can visit mine in the Smithsonian!

MULLER. You have problems, Dr. Pound. We're trying to get to the root of these problems.

POUND. I don't have any problems.

MULLER. You told Dr. Glassberg that you hear voices from time to time.

POUND. I was talking about the Muse. Just musing on poetry.

Glassberg was obviously not amused.

MULLER. We can help you. But it requires dismantling the brain, piece by piece before we can reconstruct it.

POUND. *(Alarmed.)* I got nothing more to say to you. Brother, I'm through.

MULLER. Oh, no, you're not, Dr. Pound, you have much more to say. I understand your defensiveness and even your hostility. But in time you'll come to realize, because you're a genius and you can't fail to realize, that psychiatry is your last, best hope. Because we don't sit in judgement on you, Dr. Pound. We never judge. We simply try to understand and rectify. Until tomorrow, then ... *(Blackout.)*

VOICE. URGENT TO: DEPARTMENT OF JUSTICE, WASHINGTON, D.C.

FROM: COMMANDER PENINSULA BASE SECTION, DTDC, PISA, ITALY

Reference, DR. EZRA POUND, WAR CRIMINAL. REQUEST PERMISSION FOR TEMPORARY CHANGE IN STATUS.

FROM: ALLIED FORCE HEADQUARTERS, INFO G-5

TO: DEPARTMENT OF JUSTICE, WASHINGTON, D.C.

Please advise as to current status of War Criminal Ezra Loomis POUND.

TO: ALLIED FORCE HEADQUARTERS, COMMANDING OFFICER

FROM: DEPARTMENT OF JUSTICE, WASHINGTON, D.C.

Pending further instructions continue to exercise utmost security measures to prevent escape or suicide of War Criminal DR. EZRA LOOMIS POUND. Status remains unchanged.

FROM: BASE COMMANDER, PENINSULA BASE SECTION

TO: WAR CRIMES DIVISION, DEPARTMENT OF JUSTICE, WASHINGTON, D.C.

Reference, DR. EZRA LOOMIS POUND.

Please advise. What the hell am I supposed to do with EZRA LOOMIS POUND? *(And then we are in the prison yard again. The death cages are off to one side. In the middle of a confusion of canvas*

and wooden crates is Pound clumsily and futilely trying to erect a tent. He does everything wrong, and it keeps collapsing on him. The MP enters. He has a book in his hand. He watches Pound's ridiculous efforts for a few moments before speaking.)

MP. Looks like you're coming up in the world, Old Man. Reg'lar hotel room they give you there. Reg'lar Bridal Suite.

POUND. Yeah, they finally realized there wasn't any pleasure to be had from torturing a corpse. Unless you're a necrophiliac. So they set me up with my own little *auberge*. Ain't got the hang of it yet. Where you been? Missed your ugly face.

MP. Heard you had yourself a nervous breakdown.

POUND. You heard wrong.

MP. Nervous breakdown. Thrashing around like a fish on a hook. Just 'cause they went and shot some low bottom nigger shoulda been shot years ago.

POUND. Killing off the public for my poetry's the way I look at it. Only public I got in here.

MP. Till! Who's Till? Makes me ashamed to be colored. I'd of shot him myself they give me the chance.

POUND. Picture of Christian charity and compassion, Bo.

MP. Trash like Till hurts all of us.

POUND. Oh yeah? How's he hurt you, Booker T.?

MP. We finally get a chance to do our part, earn the white man's respect, show him we belong, that it's our country too. Then along comes some trash like Till give all the colored troops a bad name.

POUND. Well not being a colored troop myself, I'm not ashamed to say I found him a credit to the Human Race, and I miss him.

MP. Anyway, you're living in the lap of luxury now.

POUND. Yeah, but I already miss the Spartan rigors of the other joint. What does Confucius say? "A handful of rice to eat, a jar of water to drink, life in a mean street —"

MP. Confucius come out of Chicago by any chance? Sounds like the way I grew up. Life in the mean streets. Shit, we didn't have it so good. Least you don't have no rats in your bedroom. Least you get three squares a day.

POUND. What's that you've got there, looks like a book.

MP. It is a book. It's a dictionary. An English dictionary.

POUND. You've decided to learn a second language?

MP. Some law against me buying a dictionary?

POUND. You *bought* a dictionary?

MP. Yeah, you wanna make something of it?

POUND. But this could be serious. Have you ever bought a book before?

MP. Naturally I've bought books before.

POUND. What kind of books have you bought? I don't mean collections of pornographic pictures, I don't mean comic books, Lil' Abner, the Katzenjammer Kids. I'm talking about *books!* What the hell books have you ever bought?

MP. You want the titles? I don't remember the titles.

POUND. *Paradise Lost*, perhaps? *Madame Bovary*?

MP. Yeah, among others.

POUND. How much did you pay for this dictionary?

MP. None of your business.

POUND. But it's entirely my business. Books are my business exclusively. Where did you buy it?

MP. In Florence.

POUND. In Florence! You went to Florence! What earthly reason could you have for going to Florence?

MP. To look around.

POUND. To look around at *what?*

MP. Pictures, churches, statues.

POUND. *(After a minute of critical scrutiny.)* I knew it. Minute I laid eyes on you, I said to myself, "This one's *ripe* for culture!" Brother, are you ripe! You don't give a damn the old girl's all clapped up, you're going to jump right in. Careful, Sergeant, I'm warning you. You think you're a long way from the center of that frozen lake, you imagine there's a whole African continent's worth of fiery real estate between you and the bottom of the pit. But once you take that first step, look out! — the rest of the way is such an exhilarating slide, you think you're flying.

MP. What are you talking about?

POUND. Hell! There some other topic? I worry about you, Amos.

MP. You don't worry about nobody 'ceptin' yourself.
POUND. Don't say "'ceptin'," Jesus Christ! "Except!" You want to be a Bloomsbury aesthete and get invited to tea *chez* Virginia Woolf, you can't go around talking the mother tongue like some coon on a chain gang.
MP. *(Dropping the dictionary on the crate.)* Here. It's for you. I bought it for *you. (Pound doesn't know what to say.)* I thought you might ... need it. In your work. *(Pound is embarrassed. At length he picks up the book and turns it over caressingly in his hands. He stands, takes up a length of broomhandle that's been lying on the ground, gives up on the tent, and strolls up and down, looking into the sky, gesturing with the broomhandle.)*
POUND. Betelgeuse. Star called Betelgeuse. Over there is Ursa Major. *(Pointing. The MP doesn't look.)* What's going on outside?
MP. Outside where?
POUND. I hear the English threw Churchill out of office. Is that true?
MP. There ain't been no change in your status. I'm not supposed to give you information about the outside.
POUND. Yeah, of course, I can understand that. You gotta obey orders. Wouldn't want it any other way. You're probably already stretching a point bringing me that dictionary.
MP. Don't tell nobody where you got it, that's all.
POUND. That was thoughtful, Soldier. My manner is a little ... a little "crusty" time to time. In general one's social graces don't improve living in a dog kennel. You could have spent the money on a piece of ass. A dictionary's a wonderful thing, even when you know all the words. Just to be able to hold it, something to hold on to, one of the few things in this world.
MP. Just keep your mouth shut about it, that's all.
POUND. What's Florence look like? How'd you pass your time? Where'd you go? What did you see?
MP. That's classified. Classified information far as your concerned.
POUND. There's a place called Fiesole up in the hills above the city. Ain't a thing on earth can match the view from there at sunset with the mists rising from the river, or at midnight, in the

full moon, when the town looks translucent, as though it were spun out of silk shot through with silver ...

MP. I liked it. It's nice, a nice friendly little place.

POUND. Old whore bitch of a city! Can't beat it for treachery. They *invented* treachery in Florence. There's a statue says it all about Florence, bird named Donatello, carved out of wood. Mary Magdalene, old snaggle-toothed hag after a lifetime of doing penance in the desert, trying to burn the sin out of her bones ... *(For a moment, he is transported on a wave of painful nostalgia.)* But there persists after everything, the curve of a breast, the contour of a thigh, the sensuality still smouldering inside — deep down — like a fire in a peat bog, might smoulder there for centuries, because of the nature of the lady's sin, the extent of it, you see.... After all that suffering, the old gal's got still more suffering to do, more expiating, before she's purified. If she's ever purified. If any of us are ever purified. *(There's a silence.)* Don't suppose you caught the Mary Magdalene?

MP. No. Didn't see nothing like that.

POUND. They're fucking with my *brain*, Kingfish!

MP. Who is? Who's fucking with your brain?

POUND. The psychiatrists. It's revenge for what they think I did to the Jews. They're trying to kill me with Freudian analysis.

MP. They're doctors. You had a nervous breakdown. They're trying to fix you up.

POUND. What do you know about these ... these so-called Death Camps the Germans were running?

MP. Not much. What I see in *Stars and Stripes.*

POUND. You believe it? You believe millions of Jews died in those camps.

MP. I dunno.

POUND. You know anybody saw one of these camps with his own eyes?

MP. No. But I saw some newsreel footage.

POUND. Yeah? Did it look authentic?

MP. I don't know. I guess so. Don't know how they can fake something like that.

POUND. You know how much I got paid for those broad-

casts? Three hundred and fifty *lire* for each one. That's about 17 goddamned bucks a week. You think a man's gonna sell his country down the river for 17 bucks a week?

MP. What did you *say* in them broadcasts?

POUND. Never mind ...

MP. I never heard you on the radio. Nobody here ever listened to you. What were they *about?*

POUND. Impossible to explain, Jim. They were philosophical things, economic theories, political science, a little of this, little of that ...

MP. Talk coming out of the infirmary, they say this is all about the Jews.

POUND. Talk's inaccurate.

MP. What's this about you and the Jews?

POUND. Nothing.

MP. I had a Jew-boy for an officer in '43. Schwartz. He told me his name meant "black" in their Yid language. He was a good soldier, Schwartz. Hell of a fighter, hell of an officer.

POUND. Yeah? Well his relatives might have owned the ghetto where you lived back in the States.

MP. We never had no problems with the Jews back home. The Jews were the only white man willing to do business with most of us.

POUND. Gouging you, sucking your people dry. The business is called usury, Amos.

MP. The pawn broker, the loan shark, they was all Jews. I don't know how my Momma woulda made ends meet sometimes without those people. This Lieutenant Schwartz was a hell of a soldier. I'd serve under a white man like Schwartz any day. That's the kind of man you can trust in battle, kind of white man you can turn your back on with a gun in his hand!

POUND. He's just another white man to you, Amos?

MP. Course he's just another white man. What is he if he ain't a white man? He ain't a black man.

POUND. *(Suddenly quoting himself.) Ad ascoltando al leggier mormorio.* There came new subtlety of eyes into my tent ...

MP. What happened? You have some bad personal experience with a Jew in your childhood? They pull something on you

personally?

POUND. *(Continuing to quote.)* Thou art a beaten dog beneath the hail, a swollen magpie in a fitful sun ...

MP. You get ripped off by some Jewish pawnbroker?

POUND. *(Wearily, evasively.)* You're out of your depth, Booker T. You're in over your head speculating about things you ain't equipped to comprehend.

MP. *(Stung.)* Oh no I ain't. You're the one in over his head! Way over his head! You think I don't know anything, you think I can't learn? You such a genius, what the hell you doing locked up in here? Maybe you belong here after all. Maybe you *belong* here with the likes of Till!

POUND. *(Trying to be conciliatory.)* Hey, Rochester, I didn't mean ...

MP. *(Exploding.)* And my name ain't Rochester! It ain't Rochester, it ain't Bo, it ain't Buck, it ain't Booker T! You been here all summer, and you never bothered to learn my name!

POUND. *(Abashed.)* Sorry, sorry, Sergeant. What ... what the hell *is* your name?

MP. Never mind! I don't know why I waste my time on you! *(And he leaves angrily. Pound, very dejected, leafs aimlessly through the dictionary for a moment and then lets it fall to the ground.)*

POUND. Thou art a beaten dog beneath the hail, a swollen magpie in a fitful sun.... Pull down thy vanity. Pull down thy vanity, I say pull down! *(Blackout. Then, in the darkness, the voice of President Truman on the radio.)*

TRUMAN. "My fellow Americans, Supreme Allied Commander General MacArthur and Allied Representatives on the Battleship Missouri in Tokyo Bay: The thoughts and hopes of all America, indeed of all the civilized world, are centered tonight on the Battleship Missouri. There, on that small piece of American soil, anchored in Tokyo Harbor, the Japanese have just officially laid down their arms. They have signed terms of unconditional surrender ..." *(Church bells pealing, the sounds of cheering crowds celebrating V-J Day. Then several bars of The National Anthem, echoed by a mournful harmonica. Then lights on the prison yard, outside Pound's tent, Forbes seated, Pound pacing up and down gesturing with his stick.)*

POUND. They say the first bomb simply eliminated the entire

city. Is that right?

FORBES. Yes, that's right.

POUND. Wonderful. Wonderful thing. One bomb, ten seconds, 100,000 Japs vaporized! Fabulous! Hiroshima. Second bomb took out Nagasaki the same way.

FORBES. Yes.

POUND. I heard on the radio, the plane carrying the second device was called "*The Great Artiste.*"

FORBES. Was it? I didn't know that.

POUND. Exquisite irony. Lovely sense of comic proportion. They say at the heart of the blast the temperature was three times the temperature of the sun. Makes a man goddamn proud.

FORBES. You have to make up your mind, Dr. Pound, how you're going to plead. They'll be moving you soon, now that the war's over. They'll take you back to the U.S. To stand trial.

POUND. What do you think? What do you think of my prospects? Not good, I suppose.

FORBES. I think there's every chance you'll hang.

POUND. *(After a moment, with some difficulty.)* How ... really incriminating are the transcripts?

FORBES. Of the broadcasts?

POUND. Yeah.

FORBES. Don't you know?

POUND. It's vague. I can't remember every damn thing I said. Memory's bad, you know. It was a time of ... a time of stress, a lot of stress and tension ... and excitement ...

FORBES. They're very incriminating.

POUND. Well, you got any ideas, Sonny?

FORBES. In fact, yes, I have. One.

POUND. Shoot.

FORBES. I think a workable strategy might be a, well, you won't like the sounds of this, but I think you might plead insanity.

POUND. Insanity!

FORBES. I don't see how else you can defend yourself.

POUND. What the hell are you talking about? Whose side you on?

FORBES. Just hear me out! A lot of important writers are trying to save you. Some very prominent people are willing to testify that you were insane even before the War.
POUND. *What?!* Who? Who's saying that?
FORBES. Ernest Hemingway, Archibald McLeish, T.S. Eliot, among others.
POUND. I don't believe it. McLeish is going around saying I'm nuts? And Hemingway? I don't believe it! How could he say a thing like that? I took care of him when he first came to Paris, I introduced him, I loaned him money! And Eliot, I showed Eliot how to write. *Il Miglior Fabbro*, he called me, he dedicated *The Wasteland* to me. You tell McLeish to go fuck ...
FORBES. These are your friends! They're trying to save your life! They think it's the only way to save your life!
POUND. I can't do it! How can I plead insanity? Think what that would mean. Who'd ever take me seriously again? My work, all my life's work ... the ravings of a madman. How do you expect me to do something like that?
FORBES. It's your decision.
POUND. In other words, you want me to rationally come to a decision to claim in court that I'm too irrational to defend myself.
FORBES. The authorities can simply declare you insane. They don't need your consent.
POUND. Then this is a government strategy. They're afraid to put Ole Ez on trial.
FORBES. The government has every intention of putting Ole Ez on trial and demanding the death penalty!
POUND. What do the psychiatrists say?
FORBES. Egocentric and bizarre, but perfectly sane.
POUND. Well, then, I'm screwed.
FORBES. Maybe not. We can always find other psychiatrists willing to testify you're insane.
POUND. *(Weakly, thinking hard.)* I think it's important to tell my story. If I don't have a trial ... I have to explain myself! These broadcasts, they're going to take everything out of context. I've got to set the story straight! It's only fair, it's only right! It's a question of fair play, Forbes.

FORBES. It's up to you.

POUND. There's nothing else? Nothing else we can do? I'm not a traitor, Forbes. Tokyo Rose, you take Tokyo Rose, that was treason! Urging the troops to lay down their arms. I never did that.

FORBES. "Giving aid and comfort to the enemy in time of war," covers a very broad spectrum of activities.

POUND. First the bastards drive you out of the country, then they hang you for treason because you left!

FORBES. Another attorney may have a different opinion.

POUND. What would they do to me? If I enter a plea of ... of insanity? What would they do to me?

FORBES. I can't be sure. I suppose they could release you. Or you could be incarcerated in hospital for the ... for the ...

POUND. In a booby hatch.

FORBES. In a psychiatric facility.

POUND. But incarcerated. A prisoner, not a patient.

FORBES. I really don't know. I can't say.

POUND. But one way or the other, the Government's going to take its flesh of Pound.

FORBES. First things first. And the first thing, it seems to me, is to try to save your life.

POUND. *(After a long pause.)* I'll think about it.

FORBES. I hope you do. Let me know what you decide.

POUND. Yeah. *(Forbes starts to leave.)* And tell Hemingway ... tell him I said, "Thanks." I appreciate his concern. Tell him I'm glad we're still pals. *(Forbes leaves. We go to black and hear a radio broadcast.)*

RADIO. And that was the Glenn Miller Band with "String of Pearls." And now, the news. In Norway today, Vidkun Quisling was found guilty of treason and sentenced to death. The Court rejected Quisling's repeated assertions that he had collaborated with the Nazis in order to save Norwegian lives. The Norwegian parliament recently voted to restore the death penalty which had been previously abolished in response to public pressure demanding the death of the traitor. In England, William Joyce, otherwise known as Lord Haw-Haw, accused also of treason in connection with his wartime radio broadcasts from Berlin, is

scheduled to go on trial sometime in October, as is Pierre Laval, the premier and Vice President of the Vichy Government. The President of the Vichy Government, Henri Petain, was sentenced to death for treason on August 15th, a sentence subsequently commuted to life imprisonment on humanitarian grounds. In baseball, Dick Fowler pitched a no-hitter yesterday for the Philadelphia Athletics.... Fowler's masterpiece was a true work of art. Although struggling with his control, Fowler was consistently ... *(The broadcast fades as lights come up to grey twilight. A wind blows dead leaves across the yard. The MP enters dressed for cold weather. Pound emerges from his tent wrapped in a blanket, shivering.)*

POUND. Jeeee-zus, Bo! I hate to see the sun go down these autumn nights. It's plain murder, the cold! *(No response from the MP.)* They're moving me, Jim. The orders came through. Going home.

MP. So I heard.

POUND. Be on your own, have to look out for yourself, Soldier.

MP. I'll manage.

POUND. Going to miss you.

MP. Sure you are.

POUND. No, it's true. I'll miss you. Little acts of kindness. Of friendship. The dictionary. The notebooks. Keeping me company. The loneliness was terrible. You take care of yourself. Get yourself an education. Hate to lose contact. I'd like to keep my eye on your cultural development. "Only one who bursts with eagerness do I instruct. Only one who bubbles with excitement do I enlighten." Confucius. Who also points out in the *Analects* that when a man is universally disliked, enquiry is necessary. And adds, "Of course, the opposite is also true." I stayed away for too long. I lost touch. It's a bad thing for a writer of poetry to lose touch with his roots, his sources.

MP. Is that the worse thing you did? To lose touch, to lose contact?

POUND. *(Groping.)* If I'm guilty of something, well, I'll hang for it. If I'm guilty of something I'll pay for it. I'm ready for that. My lawyer, he's advising me to plead insanity. It would make a mockery of my whole life.

MP. Anyway, you're not insane.
POUND. A writer has to stand by his work. The Word came before the Flesh, even in the Bible it says, "In the Beginning was the Word." The Word is all that counts. I'm a poet. It's a little late in the game to start compromising my poetry to save this wrinkled sack of blood and guts.
MP. It was just poetry then. Those broadcasts.
POUND. My conscience is clear about the Jews. I don't hate Jews. I never hated them, not the way Hemingway did, or Lawrence, Eliot, Yeats, Paul Claudel. I think there's a contradiction in an artist hating anything. I don't know how a man can create something beautiful out of that emotion.
MP. *(An overtone of the prosecutor in him now.)* So you were attempting to create something beautiful.
POUND. *(Vaguely, under obvious and persistent pressure.)* I was trying ... I think what I was trying to do was ... *(Pause.)* It's probably not a good thing to give an artist power. Or the illusion of power. There's a propensity for the grandiose statement. Pomposity. Self-betrayal.
MP. Self-betrayal?
POUND. This Jew thing.... Damned if this Jew thing ain't the most difficult idea of my life, Soldier. This Biblical Idea of the Chosen People. Can't you see it? If they are Chosen, who are we? Who the hell are *we* in the sight of God? No one's gonna believe this, but there were times I felt so close to those people in their alienation, in their exile. It's no accident I've got the mark of Cain burnt into my forehead. What the hell I end up as but a kind of Wandering Jew myself? Standing alone, despised of all men ... I went to Assisi once and crawled around the caves on my hands and knees, the caves where Francis used to pray. I was looking for the secret of Good and Evil, you see. And damn me if it wasn't revealed in those caves that the same things make a man a saint make a man a devil. He was at war with the rest of Creation, Soldier. He had declared war on the universe. Proud, intolerant, egotistical. With this perverse capacity for submission. Perversely bent on provoking the Almighty into paroxysms of cruelty and rage.... Degrading himself, abusing himself, to prove just how much he could

endure. To prove he was superior. I found in Assisi, Soldier, that St. Francis was a Jew. And I thought for a moment that I might be too. But I didn't have what it takes — to be a saint or a Jew. So I did the next worse thing and fell back on Poetry! This infernal sleight of hand. These optical illusions of a sterile intellect! I should have known better. But I was seduced, I was intoxicated by the sounds of my own goddamned voice. It makes me ashamed. Ignorance and stupidity, all the way through. *(He sits on a wooden packing crate and pulls the blanket tightly around him.)*

MP. *(After a pause.)* That's it then? That's all? That's how you're going to plead?

POUND. *(Spent.)* That's it, that's all. *(The MP produces a sheaf of manuscripts and begins to read.)*

MP. Europe calling ... Pound speaking ...

POUND. *(Startled, alarmed.)* What's that? What the hell's that?

MP. *(Reading.)* Europe calling, Pound speaking ... *(Pound freezes. He sits rigidly, hands on knees, his face lifted to the sky like a blind man listening.)* "It is an outrage that any clean lad from the country or any nice young man from the suburbs should be expected to die for Victor Sassoon. As to your empire, England, you did for a time justify keeping it on the ground that you exported good government or better government than the natives would have had without England.

"But you let in the Jew and the Jew rotted your Empire and you yourselves out-Jewed the Jew.

"You would do better to inoculate your children with typhus and syphilis than to let in Jews.

"No Sassoon is an Englishman racially. No Rothschild is English, no Streiker is English, no Roosevelt is English, no Baruch, Morgenthau, Cohen, Lehman, Warburg, Kuhn, Kahn, Schiff, Sieff, or Solomon was ever born Anglo Saxon. And it is for this filth that you fight. It is for this filth that you have murdered your empire. It is this filth that selects, elects your politicians ... " *(He turns pages, continues to read as the lights change and now the MP is in deep shadow and Pound, lit from above, sits straight and stiff like a man in an electric chair. Now, on a tape, a memory tape in Pound's head, the broadcasts in his own voice pick up the flow.)*

POUND'S VOICE. "Europe calling, Pound speaking. Let's talk about the destroyed monuments, let's talk about Canterbury Cathedral. What does Canterbury Cathedral mean to the Jew? It's not HIS Cathedral! The destroyed monuments are not monuments to the glory of Judah. They show nothing the Jew can be proud of. If medieval, they were built in open defiance of the Jew slime and the Talmud ...

"Europe calling ... Pound speaking ... The Kike and the unmitigated evil that has been centered in London since the British government got on the Red Indians to murder the American frontier settlers, has herded the Slavs, the Mongols, the Tartars openly against Germany and Poland and Finland. And secretly against all that is decent in America ...

"Against the total American heritage. But don't start a pogrom. That is, not an old-style killing of small Jews. That system is no good, whatever. Of course if some man had a stroke of genius, and could start a pogrom at the top. I repeat ... if some man had a stroke of genius and could start a pogrom up at the top, there might something to say for it. But on the whole, legal measures are preferable. The 60 Kikes who started this war might be sent to St. Helena as a measure of world prophylaxis and some hyper-Kikes or non-Jewish Kikes with them ...

"Europe calling ... Pound speaking ... " *(In the background, the tramp of jackboots begins to be heard.)*

"Europe calling ... Pound speaking. America! America! What have the English done to you? Instead of lining up Victor Sassoon before a firing squad, they dumped their criminal Jews on the U.S.A. It would have been better to send over a plague ship. A cargo of rats inoculated with tetanus and bubonic microbes. Typhus and leprosy would have been a better title to American gratitude than this pestilence of Jews!" *(Over the jackboots an enormous crowd in rhythmic chant.)*

"You have been fed on lies, for 20 years you have been fed on lies, America. And Mr. Squirmy Jew and Mr. Slimy Jew are still feeding it to you right over the BBC Radio and every one of the Jew radios of Schenectady, New York and Boston ...

"Europe calling ... Just which of you are free from Jewish

influence? Just which political and business groups are free from Jew influence, from Jew control? Who holds the mortgage, who is the dominating director? Just which Jew has nominated which assemblyman indebted to whom? And which one is indebted to Jewry or dependent on credit which he cannot get without the connivance of Jewry." *(Now Hitler screaming and over his voice and the jackboots, the sounds of gunfire, and over that the immense throng chanting "Sieg Heil!" over and over. Pound's voice grows more shrill, nightmarish, Hitler-ish. He is completely isolated now in a column of icy light.)*

"Europe calling, Pound speaking! America, America! Listen to me! You are the pound of flesh the Usurer Jew and his pimp in the White House are carving from the breast of the world. The Jew! The Jew! Disease incarnate ..." *(There is now an inferno of nightmare sounds of war: Hitler, crowds chanting, airplanes, bombs, sirens, screams.)*

"That any scum of a Jew whore in Washington should send American kids to die in the interests of his pocketbook! The Jew threatens to lower you beneath the biological levels of baboons! Take the Baruch filth, and the Rothschild filth, and the Solomon filth, and all the filth of Kikery in America and sweep it out.

"Disinfect your house, America! Scrub it, bake it, boil it, sterilize it, before it's too late!

"Europe calling ... Pound speaking.

"Europe calling ... Pound speaking.

"EUROPE CALLING ... POUND SPEAKING.

"*EUROPE CALLING ... POUND SPEAKING!" (Hitler, the bombs, the voices chanting, all pandemonium, a cacophony at a painful, unintelligible pitch of decibels now. And then a sudden silence. Pound slumps forward, as if a galvanizing current had been shut off. The lights return to normal. The MP takes out his gun and tosses it at Pound's feet.)*

MP. Here. Why don't you spare the taxpayers the expense? Why don't you shoot yourself, and spare us all the expense and trouble? *(He exits. Alone, Pound picks up the gun, and stares at it — Blackout. We hear several sharp explosions which resolve themselves into the rapping of a judge's gavel. We hear various voices.)*

VOICES. How does the defendant plead?

The defendant pleads "Not Guilty by reason of insanity."

Will you tell the jury, Doctor, what is your opinion as to Mr. Pound's ability to understand the meaning of a trial under this indictment for treason, and particularly his ability to consult with counsel and formulate a defense to the indictment.

Your honor, I think he is not capable of doing any of those things. *(Moonlight on the prison compound in Pisa. The row of cages in the compound, C., all the doors opened, the cages empty.)*

VOICE. Ladies and gentlemen of the jury, in a case of this type where the Government and the defense representatives have united in a clear and unequivocal view with regard to the situation ... *(Pound enters in bare feet, dazed, ill. He shuffles in, looks around.)* I presume you will have no difficulty in making up your mind. However it is my duty as the judge that whenever an issue is submitted to a jury to say to the jury that you are the sole judge of the facts, so when you retire to the jury room now select a foreman and try to make up your minds whether this defendant is presently of unsound mind and when you make up your minds you answer the questions that the clerk will submit to you, and if you find that he is not of unsound mind, you will return that kind of verdict ... *(Pound slowly turns to the row of cages.)*

VOICES. Mr. Foreman, has the jury agreed upon its verdict?

It has.

What say you as to the respondent Ezra Pound? Is he of sound or unsound mind?

Unsound mind.

Members of the jury, your foreman says you find the respondent Ezra Pound of unsound mind and that is your verdict so say you each and all. *(Pound inspects the inside of each cage and finally arrives at the one he used to occupy.)*

I therefore remand the respondent, Mr. Ezra Pound, to St. Elizabeth's Hospital for the Criminally Insane for care and

treatment until such time as he shall be declared able to help formulate and conduct a defense to his indictment. The hearing is now concluded ... *(Pound crawls into the cage and from inside draws the door closed. The lights come slowly down. The judge's gavel raps three times.)*

CURTAIN

END OF PLAY

PROPERTY LIST

ONSTAGE

- Cage
- 3 open-slat crates
- Canteen with water

OFF STAGE: RIGHT

- Fire hose (practical, with water) (MP)
- Double blanket with plastic liner inside
- Pup tent with 6 poles

OFF STAGE: LEFT

- Flashlight (MP)
- Bucket of water (MP)
- Food bowl (MP)
    - with: 5 bones
    - 2 rolls
- Pee can
- Tin cup (Pound)
    - with: water
    - toothbrush
- Small wooden crate (MP)
- Notebook with Chinese writing (Pound)
- Pencil stub (Pound)
- Harmonica (MP)
- Letter from notebook (Pound)
- Briefcase (Forbes)
    - with: 5 file folders with papers
    - *Stars and Stripes* newspaper
- Folding campstool (Forbes)
- Medical folder with papers (Muller)
- 2 chairs
- Dictionary (MP)
- Broomhandle (Pound)
- Dry blanket (Pound)
- Leaves

Muller's desk:
- Telephone
- Pencil cup with 5 pencils, 1 pen
- 2 books

PERSONAL PROPS

MP — Gun
- Holster and belt
- Billy club
- Key ring with keys
- Camouflage bandana
- Chewing gum

POUND — Bandage
MULLER — Fountain pen
FORBES — Fountain pen

COSTUME PLOT

POUND

Gray long-sleeve shirt
Dark gray trousers
Dirty white sneakers
Hospital gown
Brown trousers
Khaki t-shirt
Gray shirt jacket

MP

Khaki MP uniform — shirt, pants, MP armband
Black military boots
Olive MP helmet
Web belt with pockets
T-shirt
Olive Army jacket
Olive scarf
Olive half gloves

FORBES

Olive Lieutenant's uniform — jacket, pants
Khaki shirt
Khaki tie
Black shoes
Lieutenant's hat

TILL

Blacks (not seen)

MULLER

White lab coat
Khaki shirt
Khaki pants
Black tie
Black shoes

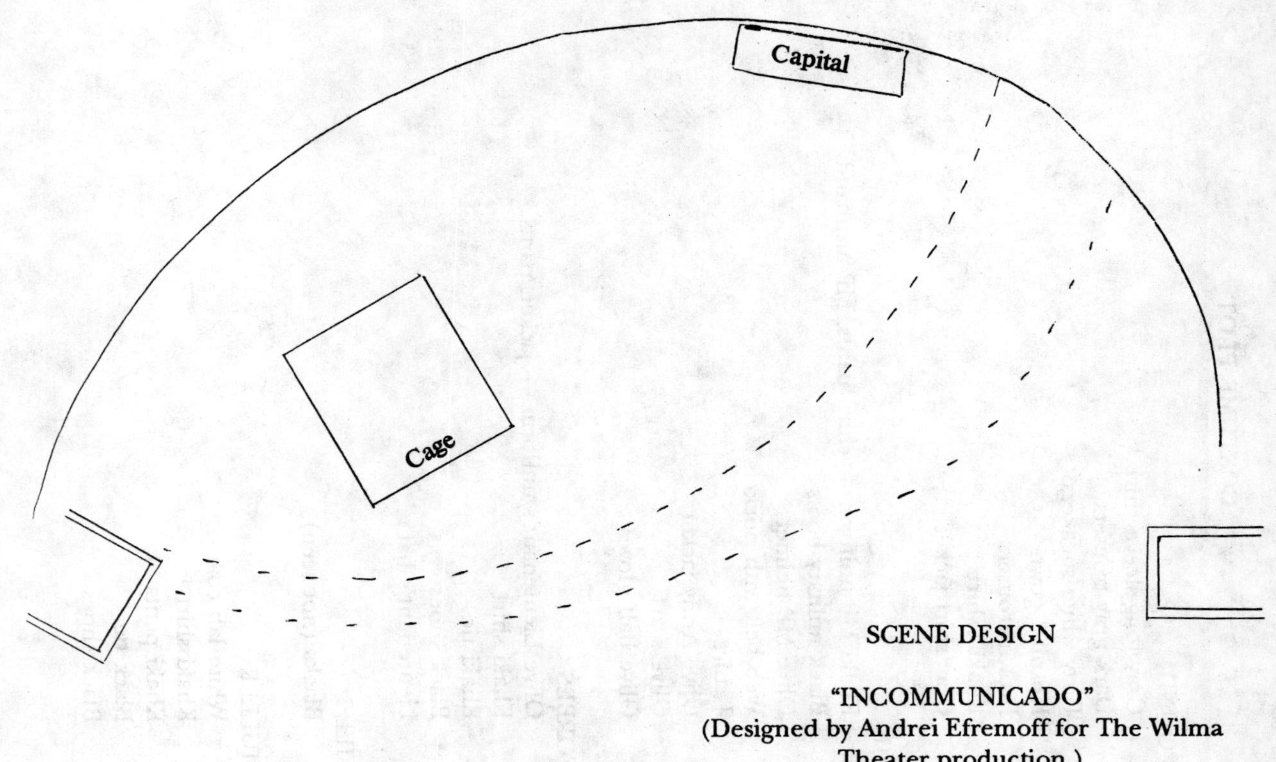

SCENE DESIGN

"INCOMMUNICADO"
(Designed by Andrei Efremoff for The Wilma Theater production.)

D1030967